REFLECTIONS ON FAITH

INSPIRED BY
BABIES

Phil Ridden

EDWEST PUBLISHING

Copyright © Phil Ridden, 2020

Published 2020 by Edwest Publishing
Joondalup, Western Australia
www.edwestpublishing.biz

ISBN: Paperback 978-0-9925481-8-6

All rights reserved. No part of this publication may be reproduced or transmitted, in any form or by any means without the permission of the author, except for fair use in worship and study.

To contact the author:
Phil@philridden.biz
www.philridden.biz

CONTENTS

Dedication vi
Why this book? vii
Why babies? viii
A word about Biblical quotes ix
LOVE 1
BABY ON BOARD 2
NAMES 4
3.00 AM 6
AWESOME 8
TOUCH 10
DRIVING 12
HOLDING TIGHT 14
LIGHT 15
PRAM 16
BABY GEAR 18
ATTUNED 20
KNOWING HER 21
REFLEX 22
PARENT 24
BONDING 26
DIFFERENT 28
IMMUNISATION 30
RELENTLESS 32
BABY-SITTER 34
SAFETY 36

THE MONITOR	38
FISTS	39
BABY BAG	40
MAN	42
REGURGITATION	44
TUMMY TIME	46
NEEDS	48
GRASPING	50
VOICE	52
PAIN	53
CALLING	54
STARING	56
SLEEP	57
COORDINATION	58
CRYING	60
ROLLING OVER	62
NURSERY	64
NEW TOYS	66
STUDYING ME	68
POWER	69
HONEST	70
TEETH	72
SOUNDS	74
PEEK-A-BOO	76
UPSET IN THE CAR	78
FOLDING HANDS	80

SOLID FOOD	82
TALKING	84
THINKING	86
SOCKS	88
MISSING HIM	90
NAPPIES (DIAPERS)	92
BANGING ON THE TABLE	93
SPLASH	94
INDEPENDENCE	96
SICKNESS	97
WALKING	98
WONDER	100
OUT OF SIGHT	102
FIRSTS	104

Dedication

This book is dedicated to Kylie, to my friend, Nina, to the babies who have enriched my life, and to the congregations who have challenged me to share my understanding of faith.

Why this book?

More than fifty years ago, Michel Quoist wrote:

> *If we knew how to listen to God, if we knew how to look around us, our whole life would become prayer. ... Words are only a means. However, the silent prayer which has moved beyond words must always spring from everyday life, for everyday life is the raw material of prayer.*[1]

If we seek God, we will see Him revealed in the people and events in our lives.

Including babies. Our observations of babies and interactions with them can challenge us to think about faith; reveal God to us; and teach us about our relationship with our Eternal Father/Mother.

That is the purpose of this book. As you read these reflections, it is likely they will conjure familiar images for you. I hope they will also help you to meditate on God and your relationship with Him.

This is not a book to be read from cover to cover. It is designed to be dipped into, sequentially or not, with favourite passages revisited from time to time. Perhaps it will inspire you to add your own reflections on the theme.

---

[1] Michel Quoist, *Prayers of life*, MH Gill and Sons Ltd, Dublin, 1963, p. 22.

Why babies?

For almost 25 years, my wife and I have been volunteer foster carers of infants. Kylie is a baby whisperer, with extraordinary patience, and the ability to sit in a chair calming a distressed baby long after her bladder screams for a break!

Some of the babies stay with us for a few months and then return to a parent or extended family member; others stay for a year or more while adoption procedures are put in place. They then go to wonderful families who are prepared to give all of themselves for a child. While some of our babies are born as normal, happy infants following a healthy pregnancy, others are born addicted to alcohol or other drugs. The pain these babies endure is unspeakable. Yet with unceasing care over several months, each baby leaves us confident that they are loved and loveable.

Effective bonding is critical, so each baby receives a great deal of holding, caressing, talking and singing, as they get to know our touch, our voices, our features. Some babies bond quickly; others take longer. Each baby is unique and each comes with their own personality and their own needs.

The baby is part of our family. Photos of all our significant family celebrations over the years include a baby. When we attend events or visit friends, there is always allowance made for a pram and a baby.

Our lives have been blessed by babies. Our faith has been inspired by babies. I hope I can share some of that blessing and inspiration through this book.

A word about Biblical quotes

A Biblical quote is included for each reflection—yet I do this with a little discomfort. It is too easy to extract verses from their context where they have a particular meaning, and to use them to convey another meaning in a different context. It is possible I have done that in this book—not to give credibility, but to help you to delve into the Bible and to seek out its truth. Forgive me if I've been simplistic. If the Biblical references are helpful, explore them; if not, ignore them.

Contemporary translations have been used. All are available (free of charge) online from various sites.

Bible Translations quoted:

Scripture quotations marked **NIV** are taken from *The Holy Bible: New International Version®*, NIV® Copyright © 1973, 1978, 1984, 2011 by Biblica, Inc.® Used by permission. All rights reserved worldwide.

Scripture quotations marked **GNT** are taken from *Good News Translation®* (Today's English Version, Second Edition), Copyright © 1992 American Bible Society. All rights reserved.

Scripture quotations marked **MSG** are taken from *The Message*. Copyright © 1993, 1994, 1995, 1996, 2000, 2001, 2002. Used by permission of NavPress Publishing Group.

Scripture quotations marked **TLB** are from *The Living Bible* copyright © 1971 by Tyndale House Foundation. Used by permission of Tyndale House Publishers Inc., Carol Stream, Illinois 60188. All rights reserved.

LOVE

Why do I love her, Father?

This helpless, demanding infant
Knows nothing but her own needs.
Incompetent to help herself,
She is forever wanting, wanting, wanting;

Yet I love her—
Loved her from the start—
    passionately,
    selflessly.

Is that how you feel about me, Father?
I'm so often helpless and demanding,
Knowing nothing but my own needs.
Incompetent to make wise decisions,
Incompetent to manage my life properly,
I am forever wanting, wanting, wanting.

Yet you love me—
Loved me from the start.
Thank you for your love.

This is the kind of love we are talking about—not that we once upon a time loved God, but that he loved us and sent his Son as a sacrifice to clear away our sins and the damage they've done to our relationship with God. (1 John 4: 10, MSG)

BABY ON BOARD

They have a baby in the car, Father?

The sign in the back window of the car —
'BABY ON BOARD' —
Announces the presence of a baby.
So they have a baby!
Why must I know?

Are they letting me know
    that they're probably tired;
        that their sleep's been disturbed night after night;
        that their car is filled with infant-regalia?
Are they asking me to not tail-end them;
    to not sound the horn?
Or are they just boasting—
    telling the world that they made a baby?

I used to wonder about 'BABY ON BOARD';
But now I'm a parent,
I think that I get it:
Since this little one came into my life,
I just want everyone to know
That my life has been
    wonderfully gifted,
    truly enriched,
    filled with unfathomable delight,
And I'll never be the same again.

It's how I feel about you, Father.
Since you came into my life,
I just want everyone to know
That my life has been
    wonderfully gifted,
    truly enriched,
    filled with unfathomable delight,
And I'll never be the same again.

When someone becomes a Christian, he becomes a brand new person inside. He is not the same anymore. A new life has begun! (2 Corinthians 5: 17, TLB)

NAMES

We gave him a name, Father,
But we know him by many names.

Along with his given name,
He is sometimes
    Sweetheart,
    Precious,
    Darling,
    Gorgeous,
    Treasure,
    Little love …
The list goes on.

Each name reflects something about him,
Or about the way we think of him.

Your son, Jesus, has many names too, Father.
    Messiah,
    Christ,
    Saviour,
    Redeemer,
    Lord,
    Emmanuel …
The list goes on.

Each name reflects something about him,
Or about the way we—or you—think of him.

Thank you that my son
> can be so many things,
> can contribute to my life in so many ways.

Thank you that *your* son
> can be so many things,
> can contribute to my life in so many ways.

For to us a child is born, to us a son is given, and the government will be on his shoulders. And he will be called Wonderful Counsellor, Mighty God, Everlasting Father, Prince of Peace. (Isaiah 9: 6, NIV)

3.00 AM

I'm struggling to stay awake, Father.

He needed a feed at 3.00 am,
And, as usual, I'm finding it difficult:
The half-light,
The half-awaked-ness,
The soporific rhythm of his sucking,
The silence of the night,
Draw me down into the luxurious softness …
    and silence …
        of sleep …

Wake up!
My eyes flick open.
Oblivious, he continues his feeding.

It's difficult staying awake,
Staying alert,
When my body,
    my mind,
        my surroundings,
All whisper lullabies.

You understand, don't you, Father?
Jesus warned his followers to stay awake,
    stay alert,

When their bodies,
    their minds,
    their surroundings,
Called them into sleep.
And as they were sleeping,
They were oblivious to the approaching danger.

I struggle to stay awake while I feed him, Father.
Do I also struggle to stay alert
    to temptation,
    and to your call,
So that I may serve you
With body and mind.

Then he returned to his disciples and found them sleeping. 'Simon,' he said to Peter, 'are you asleep? Couldn't you keep watch for one hour? Watch and pray so that you will not fall into temptation. The spirit is willing, but the flesh is weak.' (Mark 14: 37–38, NIV)

AWESOME

Being a parent is awesome, Father.

I didn't know it would be like this.
The excitement of seeing milestones achieved:
    the first smile,
    rolling over,
    sitting,
    crawling,
    walking ...
Our mutual excitement at the morning greeting
    or when we've been apart.
The pain of being away from her overnight.
The sound of my name from her lips.
The touch of her hands on my face.
The slop of her kisses.

I never knew such exhilaration,
    such pain,
    such yearning.

But you knew, didn't you Father?
You knew because this is how you feel—
    when we go away,
    when we return,
    when we call to you,
    when we reach out to you
    when we speak your name,
    when we show you our love.

So he got up and went to his father. But while he was still a long way off, his father saw him and was filled with compassion for him; he ran to his son, threw his arms around him and kissed him. (Luke 15: 20, NIV)

TOUCH

I love to read how Jesus touched people, Father.

Touch is intimate.
Touch is personal.
Touch makes a connection,
    which goes beyond the other senses.

Is that why we shake hands,
    or high five,
    or embrace,
When we meet,
    when we celebrate,
    when we want to connect?

Jesus knew the power of touch, Father.
He used touch
    to heal,
    to affirm,
    to encourage.

My baby knows it too.
He needs touch
    to comfort,
    to bond,
    to know that I am here.

Let me feel your touch, Father,
When I need to know you are near.

'Why are you frightened?' he asked. 'Why do you doubt that it is really I? Look at my hands! Look at my feet! You <u>can</u> see that it is I, myself! Touch me and make sure that I am not a ghost! For ghosts don't have bodies, as you see that I do!' (Luke 24: 38–39, TLB)

DRIVING

I barely know this driver beside me, Father.

This man usually drives like a demon,
    ignoring speed signs,
    weaving through traffic,
    pushing the limits.

Today, this man grips the wheel,
    focused,
    intent,
    mute;
Carefully scanning the road all around him;
Waiting at crossroads until not a car is in sight.

And why?
A baby has entered our lives.
A precious pink-clad creature lies
    cossetted in her travelling cocoon,
Unknowingly trusting Daddy to keep her safe.

So he drives like a hearse—
    gently accelerating from intersections,
    creeping along the highway,
    easing around corners,
    irritating other motorists!

Father, this baby has changed us both
> in ways we did not foresee.
Thank you for who she has helped us become.

You too have changed us both
> in ways we did not foresee.
Thank you for who you have helped us become.

So get rid of your old self, which made you live as you used to—the old self that was being destroyed by its deceitful desires. Your hearts and minds must be made completely new, (Ephesians 4: 22–24, GNT)

HOLDING TIGHT

She grasped my finger, Father.

She wrapped her tiny hand around it,
Her fingers barely reaching half way;
Then she held on
    Tightly,
    with a grip that belied her size.

It is ironic,
Because I am wrapped
    around *her* little finger.
She has captured me,
Shackled my heart to hers.

You too have captured me, Father,
Shackled my heart to yours.
Keep me holding on.

Hold on to what is good. (1 Thessalonians 5: 21, NIV)

LIGHT

He sees the light, Father.

Paediatricians tell us
    that he can't really see much in the early weeks.
We're a bit of a blur,
But he sees light.

The light from a window,
    the light in the ceiling,
    the light from the television,
Attract his attention.
He turns his head to look,
    and his gaze is held by the light.

You are my light, Father.
Sometimes I feel that life is a blur.
I find it difficult
    to discern,
    to differentiate,
    to distinguish.
But when I turn to the light—
    to you—
That's all the clarity I need.

In him was life, and that life was the light of all mankind. The light shines in the darkness, and the darkness has not overcome it. (John 1: 4–5, NIV)

PRAM

We were just looking for a pram, Father.

It seemed so simple.
What were we looking for?
    a comfortable capsule,
    wheels,
    handle.
How hard could it be?

But no!
One has four wheels, another three.
One is for walking, another for jogging.
One fits in the car, another may not.
One protects from sun and wind.
One comes with a bag.
One has a drink holder.
One is a shopping trolley.
One has pneumatic tyres.
The list is endless.

And then there are colours.
Pink will be lovely for our angel—
    but what if we have a boy next?
White is neutral and fashionable—
    but will it get dirty?
Dark shades are 'serviceable'—
    but is serviceable what I want for this blossom?

Do you smile or frown as you watch me choose, Father?
Not just with prams,
   but in all the choices of my life.

Help me, Father, with choices.
Teach me to choose wisely,
And to teach my child to choose wisely.

Choose my instruction instead of silver, knowledge rather than choice gold. (Proverbs 8: 10, NIV)

BABY GEAR

The preparation doesn't match the reality, Father.

We prepared;
Purchased all the paraphernalia—
    the pram, cot, car seat,
    the nappies, clothes, toys,
    the powders, creams, wipes …

We researched;
Ensured a healthy pregnancy—
    the right diet,
    the right exercise,
    the right environment …

And now it is real.
Now we have our baby;
Now we have a relationship
With this little one.

And it is different,
It is more exciting,
    more wonderful,
    more intense,
    more … everything
Than I could have dreamed.

I remember when my faith was like that:
I had prepared,
Purchased all the paraphernalia.
I had researched,
Ensured the right environment.
But I hadn't faith—
I didn't have a relationship with you.

But now it is real.
I have a relationship with you.
And it is more exciting,
    more wonderful,
    more intense,
    more … everything
Than I could have dreamed.

I came so they can have real and eternal life, more and better life than they ever dreamed of. (John 10: 10, MSG)

ATTUNED

I'm learning her cries, Father.

She cries
Because that is how she communicates,
But the cries are not all the same.
I am learning to recognise
    when she is hungry,
    when she is wet,
    when she is lonely,
    when she is afraid.

Other people are not attuned to her needs
    or to her voice.
To them, she just cries.
But I know her,
I understand her needs.

You're like that with me, Father.
Prayer is my crying.
You recognise my cry,
    and what I am saying.

Am I as attuned to your voice, Father,
As you are attuned to mine?

My sheep listen to my voice; I know them, and they follow me. (John 10: 27, NIV)

KNOWING HER

I love to watch her, Father.

I'm learning thoroughly
    her features,
    her expressions,
    her mannerisms.

I recognise when she's about to cry,
Even before it happens
    by the look in her eye,
    the shape of her mouth,
    the tilt of her brow.
I recognise her sounds
That tell me she's hungry
    or wet
    or tired.

I know because I've studied her.
I should know you like that, Father.

Learn the unforced rhythms of grace. I won't lay anything heavy or ill-fitting on you. Keep company with me and you'll learn to live freely and lightly. (Matthew 11: 29, MSG)

REFLEX

The Psalms remind me of my baby, Father.

My baby's responses are all reflex.
When he is afraid,
    or worried,
    or surprised,
    or hungry …
He stiffens,
    cries out,
    throws out his arms,
    kicks,
    blinks,
    screams.
It is uncontrolled,
Seeking—instinctively—to attract my attention.

The Psalmist is the same, Father.
When he is afraid,
    or worried,
    or surprised,
    or angry …
He cries out,
    yells,
    vents his emotion.
It is uncontrolled,
Seeking—instinctively—to attract your attention.

In the same way that I respond to my baby,
You respond to us—
With understanding and love.

Listen to my prayer, O Lord, and hear my cry for help! When I am in trouble, don't turn away from me! Listen to me, and answer me quickly when I call! (Psalm 102: 1–2, GNT)

PARENT

I'm a parent, Father.

I hold this little one,
Vulnerable,
Fragile,
Totally dependent on me
    to feed her,
    clothe her,
    protect her from all that can hurt her—
And to love her.

Who am I?
What great skills
    or knowledge
    or wisdom
Have I
To presume to take on such a task?
Yet from me she will learn
    her attitudes and values—
    including those I am unaware of teaching her.
Sometimes the responsibility overwhelms me.

Help me, Father,
    to be the parent she needs.

Help me to teach her about life;
Help me to teach her about love;
Help me to teach her about you;

As you, my Father,
Have taught me about life;
Have taught me about love;
Have taught me about yourself.

Thank you
    for being the eternal parent I need.

Fix these words of mine in your hearts and minds ... Teach them to your children, talking about them when you sit at home and when you walk along the road, when you lie down and when you get up. (Deuteronomy 11: 18–20, NIV)

BONDING

We know how important bonding is, Father.

From experience
We know that this helpless,
    dependent,
    vulnerable life
Must bond to learn to trust;
That those closest to her
Are the world that will make her feel secure.

From research
We know that this forming,
    growing,
    developing life
Must bond to learn to relate;
That if she fails to attach in the first few months,
The trauma will impact her forever.

And so we hold,
    caress,
    talk,
    sing,
Until she recognises us,
    responds to our voice and touch,
    anticipates our care;
Until she knows that we belong to her.

Why do I forget that it's the same with you, Father?

From experience
I know that my helpless,
> dependent,
> vulnerable life
Must bond to learn to trust—you.

From your word
I know that my forming,
> growing,
> developing life
Must bond to learn to relate—to you.

And this bonding can only happen
As we spend time together.

Help me to never be so busy
That I neglect my time with you.

Yet the news about him spread all the more, so that crowds of people came to hear him and to be healed of their sicknesses. But Jesus often withdrew to lonely places and prayed. (Luke 5: 15–16, NIV)

DIFFERENT

My child is different from other kids, Father.

He came into our world
As a gift
    wrapped in a shock,
    inside a worry,
    sealed with a trauma.

He will never be able to do
What other kids do—
    in the same time frame.
He will need medical intervention—
    often.
He will need intense care—
    constantly.
He will need help—
    forever.

I don't ask why.
It is the nature of life:
Our bodies acquire diseases,
    function inadequately,
        age,
        die.
Instead, I open myself to the joy
    that this little one brings to our lives.

He has taught me
 about strength,
 and acceptance,
 and life,
 and faith.
And because I realize how fragile life can be,
I treasure every moment with him,
 every struggle,
 every triumph,
 every joy he brings.

And Father,
Because I realize how fragile faith can be,
I treasure every moment with you.

I will need your intervention—
 often.
I will need intense care—
 constantly.
I will need help—
 forever.
But I open myself to the joy
 that you bring to my life.

And my God will meet all your needs according to the riches of his glory in Christ Jesus. To our God and Father be glory for ever and ever. (Philippians 4: 19, NIV)

IMMUNISATION

She's been immunized, Father.

She is now selectively protected
From common and high-risk illnesses.

As the needle went in,
She gave me a look that asked
How I could allow this to happen to her,
Flooding me with guilt.
She thought my role was
    to protect her from pain,
    to protect her from strangers hurting her,
    to ensure bad things didn't happen.

She doesn't understand that was what I was doing.
A little pain now,
To protect her from illness later,
Illness which could have life changing
    or life threatening
Consequences.

I wish I could do more, Father.
I wish I could immunize her
    from a range of other evils—
People who could hurt her,
Things that could harm her,

Her own actions which could have life changing
  or life threatening
Consequences.
Loving Father,
You placed her in my hands
To raise and protect her.

You love her as much as I do.
So I place her in your hands,
So we can do this
Together.

The Lord will guard you; he is by your side to protect you. The sun will not hurt you during the day, nor the moon during the night. The Lord will protect you from all danger; he will keep you safe. He will protect you as you come and go now and forever. (Psalm 121: 5–8, GNT)

RELENTLESS

It's relentless, Father,
Caring for this baby.

I love to do it,
But it seems there isn't a moment
When I'm not needed
    to feed her,
    change her,
    bath her,
    comfort her …
One cycle leading into another
In a never-ending performance.

I just want a hot cup of tea—
    not lukewarm, or cold, milk curdled on top.
But if I find the time to make it,
I don't have time to drink it.

I just want a sandwich—
    anything which resembles food.
But if I find the time to get it,
I don't have time to eat it.

I just want to go to the bathroom—
    surely that's in the parents' manifesto.
But if I find a moment to get there,
I am encased in the noise of this crying baby.

And the end of the tunnel slips further away,
Like the end of a rainbow.

I guess you understand, Father.
We make constant demands on you,
Complaining or criticising
    when our little world is upset,
Demanding your attention
    to solve our problems,
    and meet our needs.

Father, your love endures all things.
Sustain me with your strength.
Preserve me with your patience,
Nourish me with your nearness.
Empower me with your presence.
Compose me with your calmness.

Love is patient, love is kind. It always protects, always trusts, always hopes, always perseveres. (1 Corinthians 13: 4, 7, NIV)

BABY-SITTER

I'm conflicted, Father.

We were longing for some time alone,
A night out,
For just the two of us.
For the first time
    we have left him in someone else's care,
And we're not there.

But now I can't relax.
I hear his voice and turn suddenly
    to realise he's not here.
I check my phone to make sure it's turned on
    in case we're needed.
Should I phone to make sure he's all right?
Should we go home?
Is he missing us?
Will the baby-sitter know how to calm him?
Will she care for him as she would her own?

Do you worry about me, Father,
When I allow my life to drift
    away from your care?
When I place my trust and confidence in others
    more than in you?

I thought how wonderful it would be for you to be here among my children. I planned to give you part of this beautiful land, the finest in the world. I looked forward to your calling me 'Father' and thought that you would never turn away from me again. (Jeremiah 3: 19, MSG)

SAFETY

It's like a health and safety demonstration here, Father.

Because of our baby,
 we are excessively safety aware:
Cupboards are inaccessible.
 Check.
Doors have safety locks.
 Check.
Drawers cannot pinch little fingers.
 Check.
There is nothing dangerous at head height.
 Check.
Electronic equipment is out of reach.
 Check.
Electric switches are protected.
 Check.
There are no choking or swallowing hazards.
 Check.
Toy stuffing cannot be pulled out.
 Check.
Cot, car seat, pram, rocker, all meet safety standards.
 Check.
No clothes or toys can wind around her neck.
 Check.
There are no pillows to suffocate her.
 Check.

She must lie on her back …
    no, her tummy …
    no, her side!
Panic!
What does the latest research recommend?

Father, there is so much potential danger
From which we must protect her
    because she lacks the ability to protect herself.

Make me as diligent with her moral and spiritual safety.
There is so much potential danger
From which we must protect her
    because she lacks the ability to protect herself.

Guard my life and rescue me; do not let me be put to shame, for I take refuge in you. May integrity and uprightness protect me, because my hope, Lord, is in you. (Psalm 25: 20–21, NIV)

THE MONITOR

I'm glad of the monitor, Father.

When I am not beside him,
I can hear him:
His snuffles,
    his burps,
    his little cries,
    even his squirming around—
I hear them all;
And when he wakes,
I hear him chatting to himself,
    or singing,
    or calling to me.

Do you hear me, Father,
    wherever I am,
    whatever I'm doing?
Do you listen for my quietest mutterings?

I pray to you, O God, because you answer me; so turn to me and listen to my words. (Psalm 17: 6, GNT)

FISTS

His hands are fists, Father.

It is sign of the tension in his body.
But as he rests in our arms,
And learns to trust
    our presence,
    our care,
    our love,
He will relax.
The tension will leave him
And his tiny fists will open.

That's what happens when I talk to you, Father.
As I rest in you,
And learn to trust
    your presence,
    your care,
    your love,
I relax.
The tension leaves me
And I am open before you.

I wait patiently for God to save me; I depend on him alone. He alone protects and saves me; he is my defender, and I shall never be defeated. I depend on God alone; I put my hope in him. (Psalm 62: 1–2, 5, GNT)

BABY BAG

The baby bag is a treasure trove, Father.

In addition to nappies, it holds
    tissues,
    wipes,
    bottles,
    formula,
    clothes,
    nappies,
    rugs,
    toys,
    powder and creams …
Every conceivable item which might be needed
To cope with the anticipated
    and the unexpected.

Sometimes, Father, I wish I had a 'life' bag—
A collection of items which equip me
To cope with the anticipated
    and the unexpected.

But such a thing cannot be.
And yet …
Perhaps it can:
All I need in my bag is
Trust—
A willingness to allow you to take charge.
Then I will be equipped for anything.

All mankind scratches for its daily bread, but your heavenly Father knows your needs. He will always give you all you need from day to day if you will make the Kingdom of God your primary concern. (Luke 12: 30-31, TLB)

MAN

I love to hold her, Father.

She is nestled, warm and snug, in my arms.
    my baby.
    my child.
    my precious, vulnerable bundle of love.
I lack the words to articulate how I feel.

But I carry scars of strife.
How can I hold such innocence?
How can I raise her right?
How can I show her how to live her life?

And yet—
She does not judge or question.
She vents no condemnation.
She does not tell me that I'm not up to scratch.
Instead, she smiles at me.

So I can no longer be a boy
    reckless,
    self-absorbed.
I will be a better man than I have ever been.
I will teach her what to expect of men
    and what a man should be.

I will teach her that
>   stubble chin and heady sweat,
>   deep voice and steely muscle,
>   tattoos and hairy chest
Are not the measures of a man—

But love,
And faith,
A willingness to sacrifice and serve,
For love of her,
For love of others,
And for love of you, Father.

A good man brings good things out of the good stored up in his heart, and an evil man brings evil things out of the evil stored up in his heart. For the mouth speaks what the heart is full of. (Luke 6: 45, NIV)

REGURGITATION

It's the messy way of babies, Father.

The milk goes in,
And the milk comes out—
    regurgitated.

It doesn't hurt her,
    or distress her.
She smiles as I fuss about,
    mopping and wiping
    her face,
    her clothes,
    me!

It's like an overflow.
She can only hold so much
even of something good.

Father, I love the way the Psalmist
Overflows with gratitude
    for your goodness.
It is as though he can hold only so much
Before his cup overflows.

Thank you for your goodness to me,
Satisfying,
Filling,
Overflowing.

You prepare a banquet for me, where all my enemies can see me; you welcome me as an honoured guest and fill my cup to the brim. I know that your goodness and love will be with me all my life; and your house will be my home as long as I live. (Psalm 23: 5–6, GNT)

TUMMY TIME

He needs his tummy time, Father.

We place him on his tummy,
On a rug on the floor,
And he kicks
    and wriggles,
    and struggles,
    and strains,
As he pushes with his hands
To arch his back,
And lift his head.

He doesn't always like it,
But it is only for a few minutes,
And it matters.

It develops his muscles
So that he will be better able
    to do the things he needs to do
As he grows.
It develops his resilience
So that he will be better able
    to deal with challenges
As he grows.

Do I need to spend more time on the floor, Father—
Not on my tummy, but on my knees?

Prayer develops my faith muscles
So that I am better able
    to do the things I need to do
As I grow—
    in my life and my faith.
It develops my resilience
So that I will be better able
    to deal with challenges
As I grow—
    in my life and my faith.

The prayer of a person living right with God is something powerful to be reckoned with. (James 5: 17, MSG)

NEEDS

I'm learning what he wants, Father.

He cries—
    but every cry is not the same.
There's no great science to it.
I've simply learnt to recognise
    when he is hungry,
    when he needs a cuddle,
    when he needs changing,
    when he is ready to sleep,
    when he is unwell.
He doesn't have words yet,
But I know what he wants.

I don't always give him what he wants,
    but I always give him what he needs.

You're like that with me, Father.
You know what I want,
    even before I want it.
Better, you know what I need,
    even before I need it.
Thank you that you know my needs,
And you meet my needs.

Reflections on faith inspired by babies   Phil Ridden

When you pray, do not use a lot of meaningless words, as the pagans do, who think that their gods will hear them because their prayers are long. Do not be like them. Your Father already knows what you need before you ask him. (Matthew 6: 7–8, GNT)

GRASPING

He grasps things now, Father.

He holds them tightly,
But cannot yet let go.
So when he wants to pick up something else,
He is confused,
Because he cannot release one
    to grasp the next.

I'm sometimes like that, Father.
I hold onto things
    which should be let go.
I am hampered when I want to move on
    by what I hold onto.

Help me to let go of things which hold me back—
    enjoyable though they may be,
    attractive though they may be,
    painful though they may be,
    poignant though they may be …
So that I may move on to the future
    you plan for me.

I'm not saying that I have this all together, that I have it made. But I am well on my way, reaching out for Christ, who has so wondrously reached out for me. Friends, don't get me wrong: By no means do I count myself an expert in all of this, but I've got my eye on the goal, where God is beckoning us onward—to Jesus. I'm off and running, and I'm not turning back. (Philippians 3: 12–14, MSG)

VOICE

She's found her voice, Father.

I don't mean her cry
Nor her attempts at communication:
Now she has learnt to squeal,
To scream,
To make all manner of noises—
    loud noises,
    ear-piercing noises,
Just because she can!

Do I do that to you, Father?
Do I demand your attention
With inappropriate noise,
    loud demands,
    insistent cries?
Because I know,
In my heart, that it is not necessary;
That you know I am here,
You know my need,
You hear my cry,
Even before I utter it.

Hear my cry, O Lord; listen to my call for help! (Psalm 130: 2, GNT)

PAIN

If only I could take her pain, Father.

I know she is hurting.
Her eyes watch me and ask
'Why don't you take the pain away?'
    and I feel helpless.

If I could,
    I would take her pain into my body.
If I could,
    I would take her anguish and make it mine.
If I could,
    I would sacrifice anything for her ...
Because I love her.

Is that how you felt, Father,
    when you sent Jesus to us?
Is that how you felt
    when you took our pain into your body?
Is that how you felt
    when you took our anguish and made it yours?
Is that how you felt
    when you sacrificed everything for us ....?
Because you love us?

And Christ himself is the means by which our sins are forgiven, and not our sins only, but also the sins of everyone. (1 John 2: 2, GNT)

CALLING

I love the way he responds to my voice, Father.

I enter the room, and speak,
And he immediately turns to me.
Sometimes, he speaks,
    in the sincere vocalizations of an infant.
Sometimes he kicks his legs
    and flaps his arms with excitement.
He knows my voice
And he wants to relate,
    to communicate.

It's reciprocal.
I know his voice too.
In a crowded place,
I recognise his cry
Among all the others.
I never thought it possible,
    until I experienced it.

You call me, Father.
You speak to me in all sorts of ways.
Do I know your voice?
And do I respond—
    to relate,
        to communicate?

Because *you* know *my* voice.
Amid the clamour of the world,
I know that I am heard
When I call to you.

Make me receptive to your call—
Even when other noises threaten to drown it out.

My sheep recognise my voice, and I know them, and they follow me. (John 10: 27, TLB)

STARING

I caught her staring again, Father.

I look down at her,
Only to find her staring up at me.
It fascinates me.
Is it love?
Is it discovery?
Is it searching to understand me?

All I know is that it delights me
That she wants to explore my face
And understand my mind,
    and my heart.

I don't think I do that enough with you, Father.
I should spend more time staring into your face—
Seeking to know you better,
Seeking to search what is in your heart.
Forgive me for not staring enough.

Glory in his holy name; let the hearts of those who seek the Lord rejoice. Look to the Lord and his strength; seek his face always. Psalm 105: 3–4, NIV)

SLEEP

He's asleep, Father.

They say the joy of parenthood
Is the feeling you get when the children are asleep!
Certainly it's a joy to look at him
And hold him—
    relaxed,
    breathing rhythmically,
    an angel smile on his lips,
    his tiny hand grasping my thumb:
Totally at peace.

I could place him in his bed,
But I want to enjoy this moment;
For his peace brings me peace,
And in that peace, I find strength.

Your peace is like that, Father.
When I place myself,
    and all my troubles and weariness
Totally in your arms,
You enfold me in peace,
And in that peace, I find strength.

I am leaving you with a gift—peace of mind and heart! And the peace I give isn't fragile like the peace the world gives. So don't be troubled or afraid. (John 14: 27, TLB)

COORDINATION

She tries to grab the dangling toy, Father.

She sees it moving before her face,
Reaches out to grasp it,
    and misses.
Her hand-eye coordination is inadequate.
Yet she keeps trying,
Determined to grasp this thing before her eyes.
And then, when
    unexpectedly,
She manages to hold it,
Then she will not let go.

I sometimes feel like that with you, Father.
I want to grasp you,
To hold onto you,
To feel that I understand,
And know you deeply,
But cannot quite reach you;
You slip by just out of reach.

Perhaps I have poor faith-eye coordination;
Or perhaps it is the nature of faith.
Perhaps if we grasped you fully,
We would presume to own you,
To make you ours to control.

Perhaps you must always be a little beyond our grasp,
So that we may continue in awe of the mystery
Of you.

I pray that you, being rooted and established in love, may have power, together with all the Lord's holy people, to grasp how wide and long and high and deep is the love of Christ, and to know this love that surpasses knowledge—that you may be filled to the measure of all the fullness of God. (Ephesians 3: 17–19, NIV)

CRYING

She's still crying, Father.

She's bathed, fed, warm;
Her bed is new-made;
She's shows no sign of being ill;
Yet she cries the moment I put her down.

I feel irritation,
　　frustration …
There are things I want to do,
　　things I need to get done,
　　　but she just wants me to hold her.

Why is she so needy?
Why is she so demanding?
Why will she not let me be?

Father, help me.
Still my racing pulse;
Calm my taut nerves;
Overwhelm me with the peace
　　that you alone can offer;
And Father, grant her your peace.

Help me to show her that I am here,
　　that she is safe in my presence,
And that's enough.

And Father,
When I am needy,
    demanding,
    wanting things to be made right,
    harassing you for your attention,
Help me to know
    that I am safe in your presence,
And that's enough.

O my people, trust him all the time. Pour out your longings before him, for he can help! (Psalm 62: 8, TLB)

ROLLING OVER

He rolls over, Father.

No significant achievement for humankind,
But a significant moment in his life—
And now he wants back again.

He's not sure how he got himself into this position,
But he is sure that he doesn't want to be there.
I help him,
    gently assisting him to roll back.
Then he rolls over again,
    and the cycle repeats!
It's a stage he must go through.

Yes, Father, I know that I'm like that sometimes:
I get myself into a situation,
Then call on you to get me out of it,
    before doing it again.
I want to make my own decisions,
But I'm quick to call for your help
    when it goes wrong.

Perhaps it's a stage I must go through.
Be patient with me, Father.
Teach me,
Assist me,
Sometimes let me to sort it out,

But never,
Never,
Leave me.

The Lord himself will lead you and be with you. He will not fail you or abandon you, so do not lose courage or be afraid. (Deuteronomy 31: 8, GNT)

NURSERY

The nursery is full of him, Father.

Even when he's not there,
I go into the room,
And I feel his presence.

It's in the clutter—
    change table,
    cot,
    toys,
    drawers.
    nappies,
    clothes,
    pictures on the walls.

It's in the smells—
    creams,
    wipes,
    the fragrance of babies.

It's in the sounds—
    toys rattling,
    tinkling,
    musical.

It's in the ambience,
The overpowering feeling
That a baby lives here.
He has filled our world with his presence.

You do that too, Father
You fill my world with your presence.

I see you and hear you
    in the things that make up my world,
    the events of my day.
    the people I meet.

I hear you within me:
    speaking,
    encouraging,
    guiding.

I sense your presence when I am alone,
When I am uncertain or apprehensive,
When I am afraid.

Don't ever take your presence from me, Father.

You will show me the path that leads to life; your presence fills me with joy and brings me pleasure forever. (Psalm 16: 11, GNT)

NEW TOYS

We seem to be constantly on the lookout for new toys,
Father.

It's not that we want to overwhelm her:
It's just that she is ever growing,
    ever changing,
    ever achieving new things,
    ever needing new challenges.

The toy that once satisfied her no longer does;
The game that once challenged her no longer does;
The book that once fascinated her no longer does;
And I'm glad.

I love watching her grow,
Progressing from one stage to another—
From watching to reaching to grasping;
From lying to rolling to kneeling to sitting to standing;
From silently watching to idle babbling to purposeful communicating;
And it will never cease.

Throughout her life
Each stage will be followed by another,
Each achievement by another,
Each challenge by another.

There is a natural sequence to it,
common across all cultures.
Is my faith developing like that, Father?
Do you love to see me grow,
Progressing from one stage to another?
Am I constantly growing in my understanding
    of you,
    of the world,
    of faith,
    of commitment,
    of service?

Keep me growing, Father,
For if I cease to grow,
    in life or in faith,
I die.

We ought always to thank God for you, brothers and sisters, and rightly so, because your faith is growing more and more, and the love all of you have for one another is increasing. (2 Thessalonians 1: 3, NIV)

STUDYING ME

She studies me, Father.

She explores my face;
Staring and stroking,
As though wanting to understand
 and remember its detail;
She explores my ear with her fingers;
She examines my whiskers one at a time;
She places her eye against mine,
As though wanting to see deep within me.

And I love it!
Knowing that she loves me so much,
 that she wants to know me thoroughly.

You know me like that, Father.
And I love it!
Knowing that you love me so much,
 that you want to know me thoroughly.

Search me, God, and know my heart. (Psalm 139: 23, NIV)

POWER

She's taken control of her dummy, Father.

She puts it into her mouth,
Then removes it,
    examines it closely,
    twisting it in her hands,
And returns it to her mouth.

I think she simply enjoys the power,
The ability to control a part of her world.
It is something to delight in,
A step towards appropriate independence.

Am I like that, Father?
Do I want to be in control—
Even when I shouldn't?
Help me to know when to take control
And when to let go,
And simply trust you.

Yours is the mighty power and glory and victory and majesty. Everything in the heavens and earth is yours, O Lord, and this is your kingdom. We adore you as being in control of everything.   *(1 Chronicles 29: 11, TLB)*

HONEST

He's honest, Father.

When he's unhappy, he cries.
When we don't respond, he yells.
When we still fail to understand, he bellows.
But when he is happy,
His joy is unrestrained:
    he smiles,
    he giggles,
    he laughs,
        from the belly,
        rocking.
It is honest.

The Bible is replete with tales of honesty—
Of your servants telling you
When they are
    unhappy,
    angry,
    afraid;
When they feel your service is too demanding;
When you do not respond
    as they think you should.
But when they are grateful,
    their praise is unrestrained.

Thank you, Father, that you allow honesty,
That you allow me to open my heart to you,
To reveal the depth of my feelings.
Thank you that you understand my emotions,
And you respond
    with encouragement,
    with correction,
But always with love.

God, investigate my life; get all the facts firsthand. I'm an open book to you; even from a distance, you know what I'm thinking. You know when I leave and when I get back; I'm never out of your sight. (Psalm 139: 1–3, MSG)

TEETH

She's getting teeth, Father.

They worry her,
They irritate her,
They upset her stomach in ways
    which doctors cannot explain,
    but every parent knows!

She chews on everything—
    fingers,
    rugs,
    toys,
    teething rings,
    me!
She doesn't know why.
She does it because she must.

She doesn't understand that this is a stage of life
    which she must endure;
That teeth will equip her
    to handle solid food;
That teeth will re-shape her mouth,
    to assist her with speech;
That teeth will re-define her features
    and redesign her face.

I've been through teething in my faith, Father.
You confronted me with uncomfortable experiences
To chew on—
> difficult people,
> awkward situations,
> complex doctrine,
> bewildering challenges,
> confusing events,
> anti-Christian proclamations …

I understand that this was a stage in my faith
> which I needed to endure;

That these experiences equipped me
> to handle 'solid food' in my faith—
> difficult and challenging ideas and circumstances;

That these experiences re-shaped my understandings,
> to assist me to speak my faith,
> clearly and articulately;

That these experiences re-designed my life,
> to show your love more effectively
> day by day.

Then we will no longer be infants, tossed back and forth by the waves, and blown here and there by every wind of teaching and by the cunning and craftiness of people in their deceitful scheming. Instead, speaking the truth in love, we will grow to become in every respect the mature body of him who is the head, that is, Christ. (Ephesians 4: 14–15)

SOUNDS

I love her sounds, Father.

Squeals and squeaks,
Growls and grunts,
Chuckles and chortles,
Ba-ba, ma-ma, da-da …

They have no meaning,
Yet they mean everything.
They are sounds of praise,
All that her body
    and mind
    and heart
Can express,
Of her joy in life.

Do you feel that way when I praise you?
My songs, my words,
Do they have meaning to you?
Do you hear my sounds of praise,
All that my body
    and mind
    and heart
Can express,
Of my joy in you?

You are my God.
I am your child.
Thank you.

Hallelujah! Praise God in his holy house of worship, praise him under the open skies; Praise him for his acts of power, praise him for his magnificent greatness; Let every living, breathing creature praise God! Hallelujah! (Psalm 150: 1–2, 6, MSG)

PEEK-A-BOO

He loves to play peek-a-boo, Father.

I hide behind the couch,
Then pop up again.
Boo!
Or I cover my face with a rug,
Then pull it away again.
Boo!

He knows where I am,
Peering behind the couch,
Pulling at the rug.

Toys hide too,
But he searches them out,
Old enough to know
    that they are still there
    where they were hidden,
That things continue to be,
    even when out of his sight.

Sometimes he hides his face
Using hands to cover his eyes,
Assuming I can no longer see him
Because he can no longer see me.

You know the game, Father.
Some of your servants over the years
Have hidden behind their hands
And assumed you could not see them.
Jonah springs to mind,
Maligned for his naivety.

Yet who am I to judge?
I sometimes hide from you,
When I do not want to do
    that which you call me to do,
When your service is demanding.

If I do not look,
I ask,
Will you fail to notice me?
Will you forget me?
Will you find someone else?

Forgive me.
I am here,
Waiting to do your will.

There is nothing that can be hid from God; everything in all creation is exposed and lies open before his eyes. And it is to him that we must all give an account of ourselves. (Hebrews 4: 13, GNT)

UPSET IN THE CAR

I tried to drive with an upset baby, Father.

You saw her—
Not just upset,
But distressed—
And I was driving.

I wanted to keep going
Because we were running late.
But we stopped,
Climbed in the back with her,
Lifted her from her seat,
Held her,
Spoke to her gently,
Calmed her,
Until her world was right again.

It didn't really take long,
Before she was settled,
Asleep,
And we were able to continue our journey.

This baby—
And you—
Have taught me
That sometimes we must stop and be calm:

When things seem urgent,
    requiring action;
When I am beleaguered,
    with insistent voices;
When competing priorities
    upset all balance;
When I am tempted to rush on
    to act in haste and confusion—
At these times I need to stop,
Turn off whatever engine is compelling me forward,
And take time to be still
In your presence.
For when you hold me,
Speak to me gently,
Calm me,
My world is right again.

When I was upset and beside myself, you calmed me down and cheered me up. (Psalm 94: 19, MSG)

FOLDING HANDS

She's learning to fold her hands, Father.

I remember when she became aware of her hands,
Holding them before her eyes
Turning them, twisting them,
As though to understand them,
Or to express her feelings through them,
Like a dancer.

Then she brought them together:
First one hand over the other.
Now, she entwines her fingers,
Linking her hands together.

I sometimes fold my hands together
When I pray, Father.

For hands and fingers communicate,
Replacing words, expressing feelings;
And all of these feelings come together
When I fold my hands to pray:

The clenched fist and open hand,
The accusing finger and caressing touch,
All relax together
When I fold my hands to pray.

Reflections on faith inspired by babies Phil Ridden

The right and the left, the calloused and the smooth,
The handshake of welcome and the wave of dismissal,
All join together
When I fold my hands to pray.

Painful scars, laboured sweat, gentle grooming,
Hands reaching to forgive, palms held forward to reject,
All bless together
When I fold my hands to pray.

Hands together and apart, applauding and forbidding,
Thumbs up, thumbs down, gestures that beckon and offend,
All blend together
When I fold my hands to pray.

Fingers cross fingers, separate yet one,
Like Father, Son and Spirit,
All weave together
When I fold my hands to pray.

Give to others, and God will give to you. Indeed, you will receive a full measure, a generous helping, poured into your hands—all that you can hold. The measure you use for others is the one that God will use for you. (Luke 6: 38, GNT)

SOLID FOOD

She's ready for solid food, Father.

It's really just mush—
A step up from liquid!
She still needs the milk for nourishment,
But she needs to begin the transition
    to a wider range of food,
For food experiences which will prepare her
    for her life beyond infancy.

It's not pretty:
    she slops it,
    she spits it,
    she spills it,
    she scatters it,
    wanting to handle it herself.
And I gradually allow her more control,
As she is ready.

I'm aware that in my faith,
I've moved well past milk.
Some foods are difficult.
Some are confronted before I am really ready.
So I spit,
    I spill,
    I toy with it.

Father, as my loving parent,
Help me to transition
To a wider range of faith experiences,
Which will better prepare me to handle life
Beyond my faith infancy.

You are like babies who can drink only milk, not old enough for solid food. And when a person is still living on milk it shows he isn't very far along in the Christian life, and doesn't know much about the difference between right and wrong. He is still a baby Christian! You will never be able to eat solid spiritual food and understand the deeper things of God's Word until you become better Christians and learn right from wrong by practising doing right. (Hebrews 5: 13–14, TLB)

TALKING

I love talking with him, Father.

He lies on my legs,
    raised up, so we can look at each other.
Then I tell him about my day—
    the achievements,
    the struggles,
    the blunders,
    the incidents.

He makes eye contact,
Listens intently,
Smiles.
Then he tells me about his day—
    what he did,
    where he went,
    what he saw and heard.

That's what I hear him say.
Other people just hear
    gurgles,
    squeals,
    giggles,
    murmurs.
'He's only six months old,' they say.

But we understand each other.
I understand his unformed words,
He understands my thoughts,
And through our communicating,
    we both feel better.

Is that how it is with you and me, Father?
Sometimes I am inarticulate in your presence.
My joy and gratitude,
My struggles and fears,
Sound to me like baby gurgles—
    dis-jointed,
    in-coherent
    mumbles.
But you understand.
Thank you that you don't need fancy words
To know what's in my heart.

In the same way the Spirit also comes to help us, weak as we are. For we do not know how we ought to pray; the Spirit himself pleads with God for us in groans that words cannot express. And God, who sees into our hearts, knows what the thought of the Spirit is; because the Spirit pleads with God on behalf of his people and in accordance with his will. (Romans 8: 26–27, GNT)

THINKING

What is she thinking, Father?

I watch her
    eyes scanning the room,
    ears browsing the voices.
Her face is unusually serious,
As she processes the sights and sounds
    trying to make sense of it all.

She's not alone.
Sometimes I, too, struggle to make sense
Of things I see and hear
    on the news,
    in the shopping centre,
    at work ...
What are we humans thinking?
What are we humans doing?
Where are we humans going?
What do we dream, hope, believe?

You must wonder too, Father.
What are you thinking
    about humanity,
    about your world,
    about me?

Help me to see you in the world around me.
Help me to point others towards you.

Don't be weary in prayer; keep at it; watch for God's answers, and remember to be thankful when they come. (Colossians 4: 2, TLB)

SOCKS

The socks just don't stay on, Father.

She rubs her feet together,
    like a cicada singing,
And, of course, the socks come off.
I put them on again
    because the air is cold;
But a short time later,
They're off again.

Does it matter?
Probably not.
In any case, she's too young to be defiant.
She removes them because of her exuberance,
Or perhaps simply because she can.

Am I like that with you, Father?
Do you repeatedly try to teach me,
Only to have me go the wrong way—
Not wilfully,
    but unthinkingly,
Caught up in the joy of life,
    and the discovery of what I can do?

She will learn about life.

Make me a learner too, Father,
    of life
    and faith
    and you.

Don't become so well-adjusted to your culture that you fit into it without even thinking. Instead, fix your attention on God. You'll be changed from the inside out. Readily recognize what he wants from you, and quickly respond to it. Unlike the culture around you, always dragging you down to its level of immaturity, God brings the best out of you, develops well-formed maturity in you. (Romans 12: 2, MSG)

MISSING HIM

I'm missing him, Father.

In ways I can't understand
    I am grieving.
I've been away five days on business,
    and I'm missing him.

I understand missing my wife:
We talk on the phone.
I can picture her wherever she is.
We're accustomed to the occasional parting.
But with this baby—
I just want to hold him,
    to see his smile,
    to hear his gurgling chatter,
    to smell him,
    to plaster him with my kisses.

I want it so much it aches.
Like my memories of first love:
Whenever we were apart
I could not erase her from my mind;
She infused all my thoughts.
It's that feeling all over again—
    with this baby!

Do you feel like that with me, Father?
When I go away,
    even for a short time,
Do you yearn for my return?
Long to hear me talking to you again?

You, like your ancestors before you, have turned away from my laws and have not kept them. Turn back to me, and I will turn to you. (Malachi 3: 7, GNT)

NAPPIES (DIAPERS)

I've just changed another nappy, Father.

I wipe away the mess,
    wash it away,
        throw it away,
And he feels fresh and clean again.

I sometimes think it would be wonderful
If I could deal with the messes in my life that way.
To wipe them away,
    wash them away,
        or simply throw them away.

Sometimes I forget that you do that for me, Father.
Through the sacrifice of Jesus,
You take my messes,
And wipe them away,
    wash them away,
        throw them away,
To make me feel fresh and clean again.

If we confess our sins, he is faithful and just and will forgive us our sins and purify us from all unrighteousness. (1 John 1: 9, NIV)

BANGING ON THE TABLE

I've taught him to bang on the table, Father.

He sits on my knee
    and slaps the table with his hands,
    delighting in the noise,
    and the feeling,
    and my encouragement.

I remember when he couldn't command his hands this way,
When he kept his fists closed;
Then when he placed his hands on mine,
Laughing while we banged the table together.

Just a little step in his life,
And yet, so wonderful—
    to me and to him.
We share the joy and pride.

Father, I think you feel this way about me,
When there is growth in my faith:
Just little steps,
And yet, so wonderful—
    to me and to you.

But grow in spiritual strength and become better acquainted with our Lord and Saviour Jesus Christ. (2 Peter 3: 18, TLB)

Phil Ridden   *Reflections on faith inspired by babies*

SPLASH

She's discovered splashing, Father.

In the bath or pool
    she flaps her arms,
    kicks her legs,
    splashing water everywhere—
Mostly on me!
There is simple delight in the experience …
Until a splash envelopes her face.
She gasps,
Eyes open wide,
As she recovers her breath.

I hold her,
Reassure her,
Gently wipe her eyes.

And then she laughs
And does it all again.

Am I like that, father?
When I discover a new experience,
A new sensation,
Do I get carried away with the delight,
Ignoring the consequences,
Until my own actions cause me to suffer?

And do you hold me,
Reassure me,
Gently wipe my eyes?

Teach me, Father,
    to love life,
    to love new sensations,
But to recognise when my pleasure
    is causing me pain.

Do not cling to events of the past or dwell on what happened long ago. Watch for the new thing I am going to do. It is happening already—you can see it now! (Isaiah 43: 18–19, GNT)

INDEPENDENCE

She can't wait to be independent, Father.

To reach her toys,
    she began by twisting,
    wriggling her way around the mat.
Then she rolled,
    randomly at first,
    then with purpose.
Now she crawls.
    setting her eye on what she wants
    and pursuing it.

The cupboards are now locked.
The bookshelves are now empty.
The remote controls are out of reach.
The DVR is covered.
Nothing is safe
    unless we have placed it out of reach.
She doesn't know that it's partly to protect our things,
And partly to protect her—
To keep her safe in our love.

Are we like that, Father?
We can't wait to get moving,
    to touch things which are unsafe,
    to get into places we ought not to go.
Keep me to stay safe in your love.

The Lord protects the helpless; when I was in danger, he saved me. (Psalm 116: 6, GNT)

SICKNESS

Our baby is ill, Father.

Not only ill,
    but suffering.
She hurts, she pains, she suffers,
    and I suffer to.
Every time I see her face contorted,
Every time I hear the sounds of agony,
Something rips at my insides.

If I could suffer for her,
    I would.
She clings to me for comfort,
And as I hold her,
I want to squeeze the hurt out.

Father, I do not need to squeeze:
I need only to pass your power through
    to quieten her,
    to comfort her,
    to heal her.
Fill her with your strength,
Your life.

At sunset, the people brought to Jesus all who had various kinds of sickness, and laying his hands on each one, he healed them. (Luke 4: 40, NIV)

WALKING

Today she walked, Father.

It was hesitant,
Yet exhilarating.
You could see it in her face—
    and mine!
We celebrated
    a new achievement;
    a new stage;
    a new independence.
And as the years go by,
She will move on,
    to run,
    skip,
    jump,
    dance …
New achievements;
New stages;
New independence.

Father, sometimes it seems
    that I am still taking my first steps
In faith—

When I first said,
'Here I am, Father,
    I will let go and step out to you,'

My first steps were hesitant,
    yet exhilarating.
But sometimes I feel like
    I haven't moved on.

Help me to grow in faith,
So that I may
    run,
    skip,
    jump,
    dance …
In faith.

But grow in spiritual strength and become better acquainted with our Lord and Saviour Jesus Christ. (2 Peter 3: 18, TLB)

WONDER

I am overwhelmed, Father.

I cannot believe all she has learnt,
    done,
    achieved,
    become,
In just one year.

It's there
    in the photos,
    the journals,
    the memories,
    the stories;
Each great and small achievement.

I think my friends may be bored at my tales
    of her latest exploits,
    her latest triumphs.
But I cannot suppress my joy and wonder
At all she has done,
And all that she is.

Sometimes I'm overwhelmed by you, Father.
When I think of your great works,
    all you have done,
    all you are,
I cannot suppress my joy and wonder.

None can compare with you; were I to speak and tell of your deeds, they would be too many to declare. (Psalm 40: 5, NIV)

OUT OF SIGHT

I was only gone a moment, Father.

I didn't even leave the room,
But I was out of his sight,
    and he cried.

He wants me to be in his range of vision
    always.
When he loses sight of me,
    he worries,
    he thinks he is alone,
    he assumes that I have left him.
He will learn that,
    even when he cannot see me,
I am still here.

I'm like that with you, Father.
Sometimes it seems I cannot see you,
    and I need the reassurance of your presence.
Help me to learn that
    even when I cannot see you,
    even when you seem far away.
You are still here.

Where can I go from your Spirit? Where can I flee from your presence? If I go up to the heavens, you are there; if I make my bed in the depths, you are there. If I rise on the wings of the dawn, if I settle on the far side of the sea, even there your hand will guide me, your right hand will hold me fast. (Psalm 139: 7–10, NIV)

FIRSTS

I've loved all her firsts, Father:

First smile;
First rollover;
First crawl;
First sitting;
First walking;
First words;
First … everything!
I've loved it all.
I have photos of each moment.
We recall them as we reminisce.

Do you feel that way about my firsts, Father?
Do you recall
The first time I tried to read your word;
The first time the story of Jesus touched me;
The first time I reached out to you;
The first time I committed my life to you;
The first time I placed my future in your hands;
The first … everything?

And do you smile as you remember?

So don't worry at all about having enough food and clothing. … Your heavenly Father already knows perfectly well that you need them, and he will give them to you if you give him first place in your life and live as he wants you to. (Matthew 6: 31–33, TLB)

By the same author:

Reflections on faith inspired by children
Reflections on faith inspired by seniors
Reflections on faith inspired by men
Reflections on faith inspired by COVID
Faith around the barbecue (The story)
Faith around the barbecue (The play)

www.philridden.biz

www.ingramcontent.com/pod-product-compliance
Lightning Source LLC
Chambersburg PA
CBHW070433010526
44118CB00014B/2031